Date Due

0

Dashwood April 15

ORR ON ICE

ORR
ON ICE

By

BOBBY ORR
With Dick Grace

Prentice-Hall, Inc., Englewood Cliffs, N. J.

CREDITS

Photography—Favero, Danny Goshtigan, Dick Grace, Leonard Lee Lester, Don Newcands, James Pauk, Al Ruelle, Thompson

Hockey Players—Ray O'Malley, Bob Rowe, Bob Walton, NHL Teammates, and Other Players

Orr on Ice by Bobby Orr, with Dick Grace
© 1970 by Bobby Orr and Richard Grace

ISBN 0-13-642827-4

Library of Congress Catalog Card Number: 79-117498

Printed in the United States of America   T

Prentice-Hall International, Inc., London
Prentice-Hall of Australia, Pty. Ltd., Sydney
Prentice-Hall of Canada, Ltd., Toronto
Prentice-Hall of India Private Ltd., New Delhi
Prentice-Hall of Japan, Inc., Tokyo

THIS BOOK IS DEDICATED TO
ALL THE ORRS OFF ICE

Arva, Doug, Pat, Ron, Penny, Doug Jr. and Elsie
Orr; to my grandfather, the late Robert Orr;
Al, Nancy, Alan, and Jill Eagleson; and Richard G.

CONTENTS

TO READERS OF THIS BOOK

Orr on Ice is a book about my experiences in professional ice hockey. It is in no way a detailed report on my career, nor does it tell everything there is to know about the game. This book is just my effort to pass along some of the finer aspects of the game.

Believing that pictures tell a better story than words, I am presenting this book to you with as few words as possible. To write a lengthy report would leave many youngsters out in the cold on the major points of the sport. Hockey is all action, and action photos speak louder than words.

Each picture section in the book is begun with a short statement explaining in simple detail the accompanying photographs.

Orr on Ice is the way I play hockey!

BOBBY ORR

7

EQUIPMENT

From the time boys first start to play hockey, a full set of equipment should be used. Injuries occur too easily. You never know how they will come about, so proper gear will lessen the chances.

Never wear loose equipment. Everything should fit snugly on your body. I wear my own equipment as tight as I can without it interfering with blood circulation. It is the only way I feel comfortable when playing. Pay special attention to your skates, which should be taut.

If playing defense, you should attach ankle guards to your skates. You need to protect your feet against low shots that might break your ankle.

I am often asked about helmets. Yes, they should be worn at all times by youngsters on the ice. In the NHL most of the players just do not like to wear them. Many claim they hinder vision and are too hot. But unless you are in the NHL, wear a helmet. Don't take chances. Even in the NHL, I feel that eventually most of the athletes will be using headpieces.

Proper drying and airing of equipment is necessary. Immediately after use, everything should be hung and dried with care and skates wiped clean to prevent rust.

Your skates should feel comfortable and fit perfectly. I wear skates as small as possible—they actually fit like a glove. I tie the laces extra tight. I am extremely hard on skates. During the season I will run through three or four pairs, sometimes even five. Before every game and most every practice I have my blades sharpened. Always remember to keep your blades in good condition. Many injuries are due to dull skates. If your blades wear down from too many sharpenings, new ones can be easily attached to your old boots. This will keep you from having to break in a new pair of boots.

9

Underwear should be worn to absorb excess perspiration; and the cup is used to prevent injuries.

Stockings come on next.

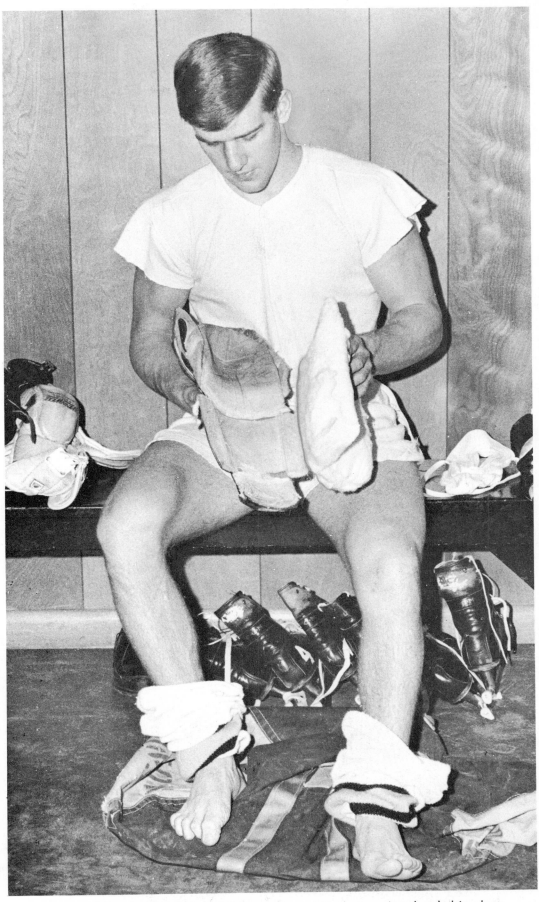

Cotton padding inside shin pads gives extra protection against hard shin shots.

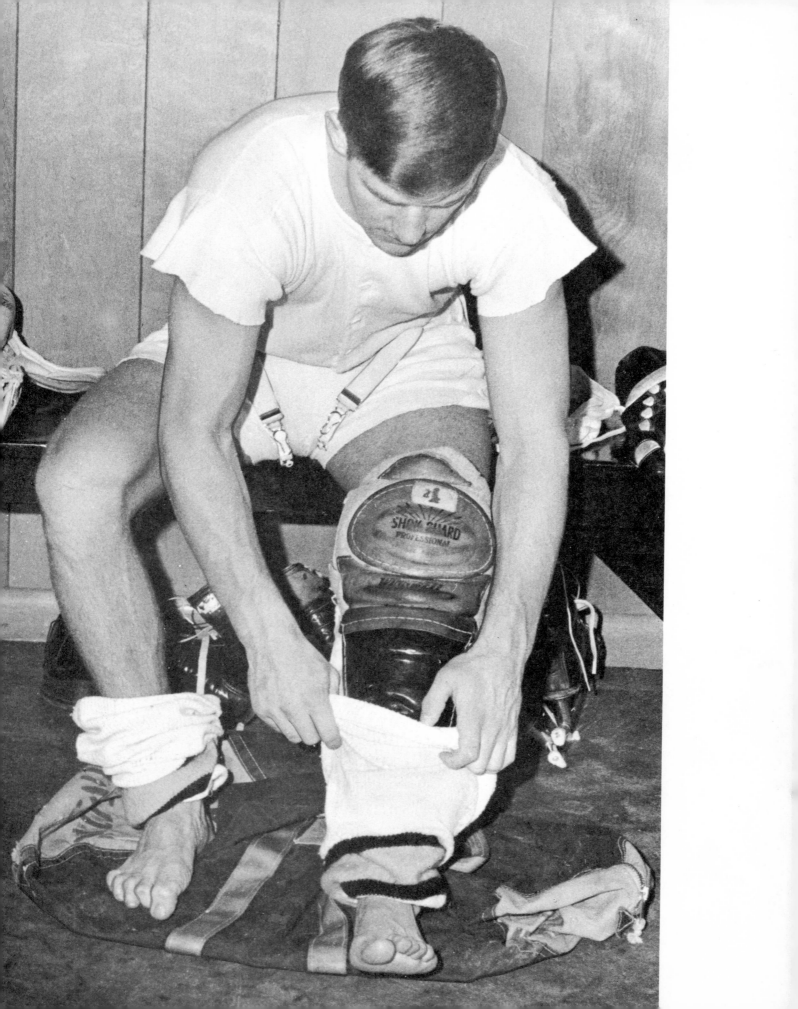

Garter belts are used to hold the stockings.

The shin pads are strapped on under the long stockings.

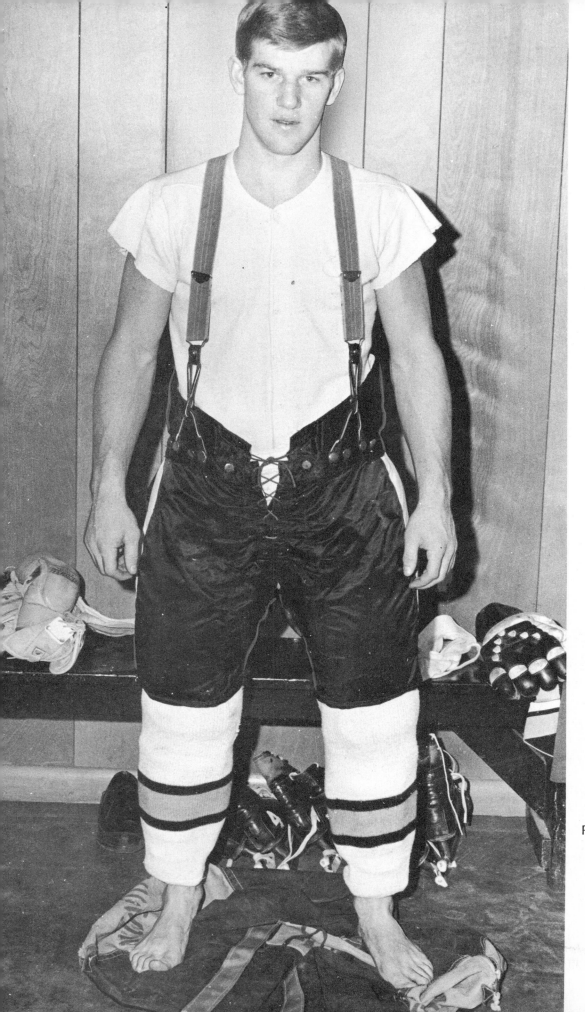

Pants go on next with suspenders.

Skates should be tied tightly and the blades constantly sharpened to prevent injuries caused by dull blades.

Shoulder pads are always worn—no youngster should ever play without **them**.

Defensemen wear ankle guards to ward off low shots that could break an ankle.

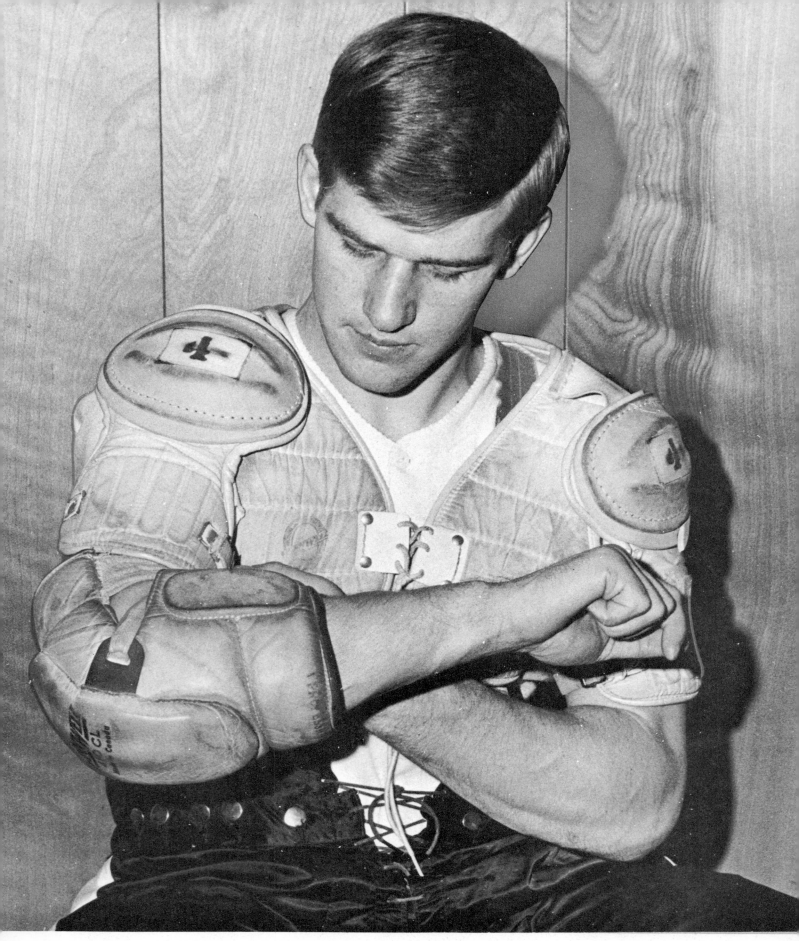

Elbow pads are a must to prevent injuries.

The team jersey completes the uniform.

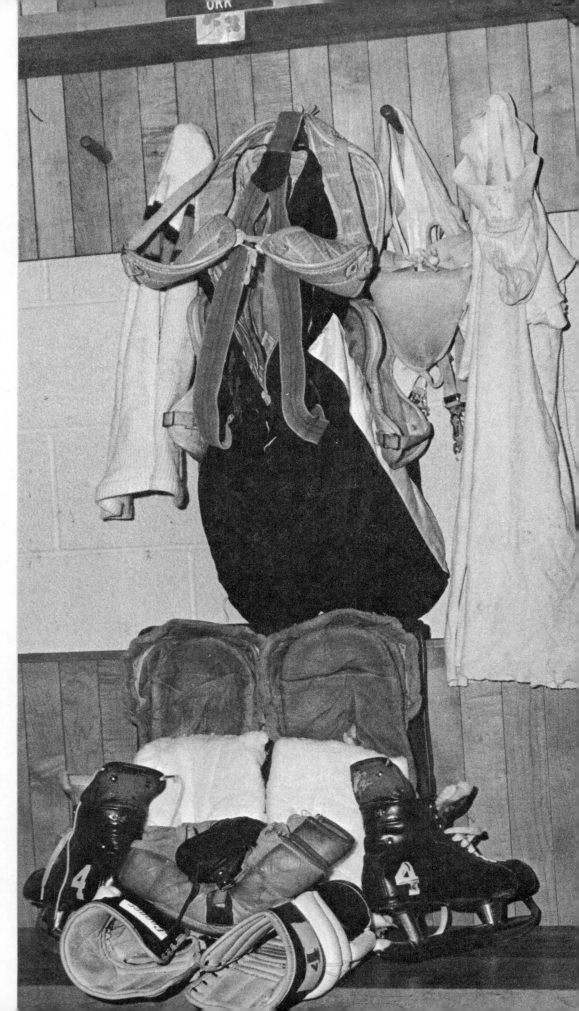

20

There is only one way to hang and dry equipment.

EXERCISES

A hockey player must exercise constantly to keep in condition and to prevent muscular injuries. Players can suffer serious muscle pulls because they did not warm up properly. This goes for all sports-—baseball, football, basketball. Muscles must be loose. If they are not, they will rip or pull. Then you are out of action.

Early in the hockey season, groin injuries seem to be the common ailment. I remember one summer game in Winnipeg when I was not in shape and had not skated since the first of April. Out on the ice, and out of condition, I got hit and tore ligaments in my knee. A freak accident, but if I were properly conditioned it would not have occurred.

Before any NHL contest we have a 15-minute warmup on the ice just to loosen up before actually playing. Let's call it preventive medicine. Make sure you do it too.

21

22

Leg kick-up exercises loosen up all the leg muscles. Keep repeating the motion —one leg up, then the other. Kick as high as you can.

23

Another groin exercise—pull leg toward your body; do one leg then the other.

24

Running in one spot—good for strengthening legs, good for balance, good for wind, good for everything.

The groin stretch. This muscle-builder gradually stretches the groin. Do both legs.

This pushup exercise is done twelve months a year. A body-molder for the shoulders and arms.

Situps are for the stomach and back muscles.

Loosen up back muscles with bends. Keep your arms straight, bend back, bend down, bend sideways.

PUSH AND HOLD

Push and hold exercises are very good. Two players get together, one pushing and the other holding. Using the same stick, one player shoves the other across the ice. The man not pushing drags his feet trying to hold the presser back. The pushing player has to vigorously dig and shove with all his strength. As you go through the workout, you will feel the results in your legs—and strong legs are needed in hockey. Without a doubt, the push and hold is the best leg and groin strengthener and an excellent way to increase stamina. This same exercise should be developed to improve backward skating.

Push and hold for strengthening legs and groin.

One man pushes, the other holds, using the same stick.

OFF-SEASON CONDITIONING

Three or four weeks before our Bruins' training camp opens, I gradually step up my conditioning program. I run a little more, do a few extra exercises. It is an overall loosening-up program.

But in the off-season I do not believe you should overdo it. Rest your body as much as possible because the hockey year is long and tiring. It is possible to get yourself down too fine with too much conditioning. Our team has a full month of training camp in the fall that gives me plenty of time to get in condition. You should reach your physical peak when the season actually starts in October.

Athletes should always watch their weight and take care not to overeat. I am very lucky, since my weight always remains the same. But for some NHL players, weight is a big problem. Those who put on excess poundage have to work that much harder in training camp to get rid of 5 to 10 pounds. Avoid pastries at all times. You will never see professional athletes filling up on sweets. Steak and other meats are standard for many of us who play hockey for a living, and so is milk. In the dressing room we have coke, ginger ale, and orange juice. After practice or a game, most of the fellows go for orange juice as a quick refresher.

If you have a weight problem, working out on a bike in a sweatsuit is helpful. A few brisk bike sessions and the extra pounds will melt off. The exercise bike is also great for knee injuries. When I hurt my knee, I immediately went to the bike. There is nothing better than pedaling a bike to strengthen legs.

A few minutes a day with the weights keeps you in off-season shape.

Orange juice is a great refresher.

Working out on the exercise bike after a knee injury.

TRAINING CAMP

Our season is a tough grind when you consider we play ten or twelve exhibitions, 76 league games, and a possible 21 playoff contests. So, about two weeks before reporting to training camp, I concentrate on loosening-up exercises—pushups, situps, running, lifting a few weights. But I try not to overdo it. Just enough conditioning to keep everything loose.

The usual camp training day kicks off at 8:15 a.m. with calisthenics. These are for general loosening-up purposes. When we get on the ice we do others—sprints, groin stretches, etc. Gradually the pace steps up every day until your wind improves and you work yourself into shape.

A few team scrimmages are arranged. Then on the tenth or twelfth day, exhibition games with other NHL clubs get under way. New players called up for tryouts are given every opportunity to show their stuff. Some stay with the club. Others are sent to Bruin farm teams for further work.

After our Canadian camp the club returns to Boston, where we work out for another week or so, and play one or two more NHL exhibitions. Then it happens—the first face-off of the regular season. Another year is on ice.

34

STICKS

Hockey sticks cannot exceed 55 inches from heel to end of shaft. Blade limits are 12½ inches by 3 inches. Sticks weigh from 17 to 24 ounces. Naturally, blades are curved to accommodate right- or left-handed shooters.

I do not recommend curved sticks for youngsters just starting out in the sport. After they get some experience, they can switch to a curve. A large curve makes it hard to control the puck. It will roll off your blade. It is also difficult to receive a pass and to make a backhand pass. Your shooting will be handicapped, as you will find the puck tends to rise too high. I do not use a large curve. My stick has just a slight hook, or what I call a good lift.

You will see many of the NHL pros with curved blades, but don't forget they have practiced many an hour before using them in a game.

There are no two players in the NHL with the same stick knobs. Some like them large, others small. Some players like to run their tape way down the stick handle, but others put just a bit of tape at the top. My own sticks carry a very large knob.

What is proper stick length? Mine comes up around my chin. Most players go along with this. But a few cut their sticks down. Stick length is really a matter of personal comfort. I skate in an upward position, so I use a longer stick with a number 5 lie. Other players, who skate in more of a bent-over form, carry shorter sticks. Find what's best for you and stay with it. Just remember, if the stick's too long it will be very difficult to handle.

How long does a stick last? That depends. I run through ten to fifteen dozen a season.

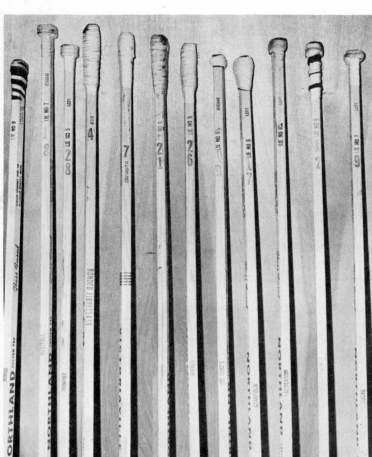

Every NHL player tapes his own stick handle in a different manner.

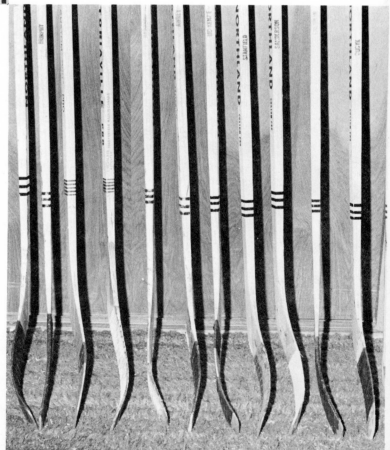

Stick blades vary greatly from player to player.

SKATING

Skating is the most important part of hockey. If you can skate, you can learn to play hockey. Look around the NHL. You will see that there are no two players who skate alike. Some take long strides while others use a short, choppy motion. It is your own individual physical convenience that determines how you skate. Some bend over more than others. Some prefer to skate in a straight-up position.

Strong legs are a must. They carry you forward, backward, and sideways, and enable you to make sudden stops and starts. Hockey is a sport of split-second action. Your legs must be able to turn properly and quickly in any direction.

The skating stride comes first. When skating you have to have a slight bend to your knees. The bend gives you good balance and keeps you from being knocked off your feet. If you stand stiff-legged and you get hit, you are going down. Now with the slant in your knees, lean your body forward and start your stride. Do not lean back and try to skate—it will not work.

When I am in my stride, my back foot is used for pushing. Always push with the rear foot. Then bring the other foot forward. Push again with the back. Just keep repeating this motion. The harder you push, the faster you will skate.

Skating exercises must be done continually by all beginners. Everyone should learn to skate in circles—crossing legs both ways, and traveling both ways, left and right. One way will seem harder than the other but keep at it. Do left circles, then right ones. Practice makes perfect. You will never get to be perfect, but you will get better.

Novices have to learn proper balance because without body balance you will not be able to skate or play hockey.

Here are two good exercises for body equilibrium. Work out running on skates, stopping, then running in one spot. Keep lifting your feet up and down. Kicking the legs is another first-rate exercise. Kick one leg out, then the other. This way you will find yourself standing on one leg, which is bound to improve your balance.

Walking sideways is another good drill. I usually have youngsters face front with toes pointed ahead. Then I teach them to place one foot over the other and walk back and forth up and down the ice. This exercise helps your cross-over movements.

In stopping, one- and two-skate stops are used. With the two-skate stop you lean backward and both your blades push forward and cut sharply into the ice to stop. It is exactly the same way with one skate; only one foot is doing the stopping. Practice both types because you must be able to stop on a dime and get going again in a flash.

Skating backward is very similar to skating forward. Your knees are together and slightly bent. Here the motion of your hips comes into play. It is the hips that give you the backward speed movement. You move by throwing your body from side to side almost like a duck waddling.

Learning to stop properly is a necessity when skating backward. You must be ready to stop quickly and go back to forward skating right away. Hockey players must be able to turn fast in both directions. If a man goes by you on one side, you have got to turn and move toward him. If it is your right side, turn your right skate to him and push off with your left to gain speed fast enough to catch the man. Should he go by on your left, naturally it is your left skate that turns toward him and you push off with your right foot.

Skating sideways is a must for all defensemen. When you are defending, you will be called upon to operate sideways after a man. Remember, when you turn your skate toward your opponent, dig in real hard because he will be traveling at a fast clip and you must go even faster to stop him.

A crossover is simply putting one leg over the other. When turning corners do not glide—skate! If you glide you will not be fast enough for executing corner and net movements. In a hockey game, things change so quickly that a second or two lost in gliding could cost you a goal, a game, or even the Stanley Cup. The thing to remember in the crossover is that pushing gives you speed.

Stick-handling could be called agility skating. Agility skating is nothing but a series of quick body changes. When you are stick-handling, you must be able to move suddenly one way or the other. This is where your feet make the difference. You have to learn to change direction very fast if you are deking (faking) another player and he catches on to your deke. Stick-handling is all in your feet and your ability to switch your skating stride from side to side.

Coming down ice, cutting in on the net.

Going around the defense, still zeroing in on net.

My man is almost beaten as I slide by him.

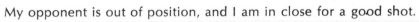

My opponent is out of position, and I am in close for a good shot.

Side view showing skating stride—knees bent, body forward, pushing off on back foot, going into full stride.

Front view—pushing off hard with back foot.

Going into a left lateral
movement, illustrating
a crossover.

Another left lateral move.

Very important for all
defensemen — lateral
moves. This one is to
the right.

43

Right lateral.

Skating around corners in a right direction.

Still going right around **corners**.

Close-up of feet executing round corners—going right.

Now a crossover going the other way—left.

A further execution of the left-direction crossover.

Skates up close in a left crossover.

45

Chairs come in handy when practicing cutting in on net and going around a man.

CUTTING IN ON NET

Practice with chairs for cutting around men. Line them up on the ice with various spacing and think of them as actual opposing players.

As you can see from the photos, I am keeping the puck away from my man so he cannot hit my stick. Note also that my arms are away from him.

In the second photograph I am cutting in. My body is leaning against my man, and I am pushing hard to get in behind him.

Always lean one way and push with the outside skate. When you are going in the other direction, lean the other way and again push with your outside blade.

To cut around men you have to be real fast. So practice with the chairs— leaning and pushing, leaning and pushing. It is the only way to learn to do it.

47

Another demonstration of how to go around a man.

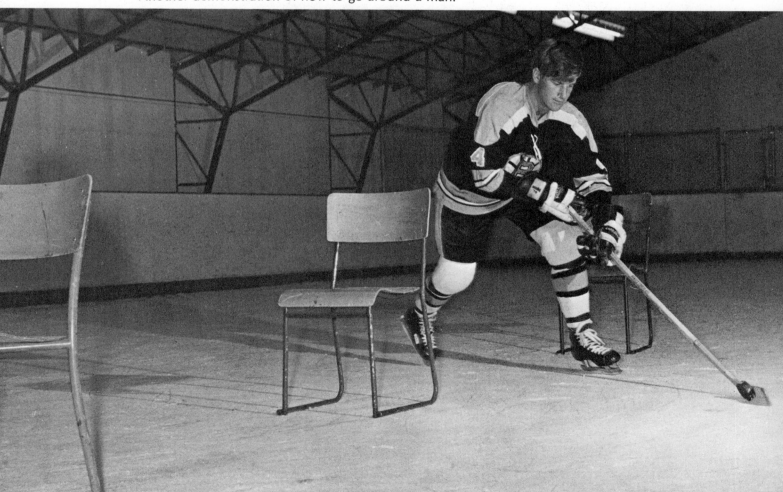

Proper method for stopping with two feet showing blades cutting sharply into the ice.

SHOOTING

You can never get enough practice shooting. I have actually spent hundreds of hours on the ice perfecting my shooting technique. The more you practice, the better you'll shoot, and more goals will start coming your way.

WRIST SHOT

As you can see in the pictures, I have set up a right and wrong way for the wrist shot. In the "no-no" photo I am leaning away from the shot. Do not do this because you are not able to put any steam into your shot. Your weight has to go into every shot to make it hard and accurate. I also have my head down, so I do not know where I am shooting.

Right way. Here my head is up and wrists cocked. Notice the position of the puck. I have my stick cupped over it near the middle of the blade. All my weight is going into my front foot. Now I have released my wrists and taken the shot. I am still looking in the direction I am shooting, and I have followed through with my stick. This will help to keep your shot lower and give you greater accuracy.

Things to remember. Hold your stick firmly—loosely held sticks give bad results. Cock your wrists. Look where you are shooting. Put all your weight on the front foot. Be sure to cup the puck properly in the middle of your stick blade. Then throw your body into the shot and complete the follow-through.

SLAP SHOT

Very few hockey players who use the slap shot use it with accuracy. Of course, Bobby Hull and others can do it, but they are exceptions. I use it myself, but frankly I feel I cannot shoot it with exactness. The slap shot is tough to master, so I suggest that youngsters forget all about using it. Try to develop a good wrist shot, which is more valuable in hockey.

Correct position for setting up a wrist shot.

The follow through of a wrist shot.

This is a "no-no" photo: my head is down before attempting a wrist shot.

A wrong way—my weight is on the back foot and I am leaning away from the shot.

Here is the backhand—weight on front foot. I am looking for an opening to shoot and then I follow through completely.

BACKHAND SHOT

You use the same procedure as the wrist shot: cock your wrists, cup the puck, put your weight forward. It is a forehand shot, except that you are shooting backward. When I finish my shot, the bottom hand is on top of the stick and I have followed through.

The flip shot—puck on toe of the stick blade and I am looking straight ahead.

FLIP SHOT

The flip shot carries authority close in around the goal when you are pressed for shooting room or if the goaltender is down.

Often the flip shot will be used to give a teammate a pass when an opposing player is attempting to block the pass by laying his stick flat on the ice.

Look at the pictures.

56

Follow-through position for a correct flip shot.

Practice the flip shot by shooting over a stick flat on the ice.

A good flip shot requires skill——keep after it.

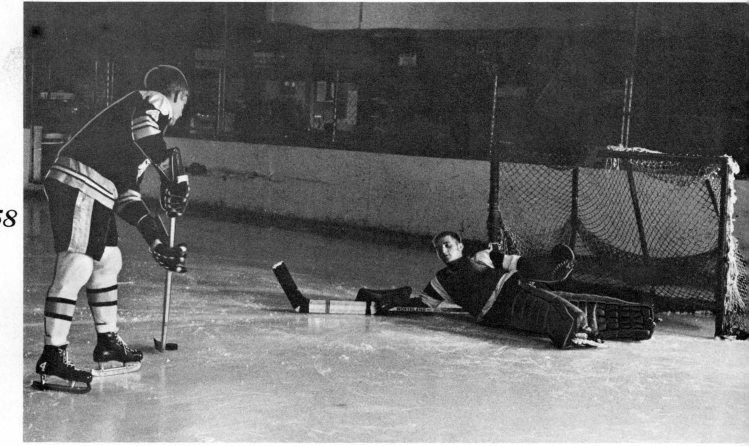

The goaltender is down out of position—use the flip shot here.

Up and over and into the net—a goal.

Four places to shoot on the net—all corners, upper and lower.

SHOOTING ON THE GOAL

There are four major spots for shooting at the net. As marked on the photo, you will see the puck going high on the right and left corners. The two lower corners are the other best spots for a shot. Hit these places and make the goaltender work for any save he makes on you.

STICK-HANDLING—PASSING

Stick-handling is one of the game's finer arts. There are three basic methods of carrying the puck: side to side, diagonal, and back to front. It's hard work but they can all be mastered with continuous exercise.

In stick-handling always tap the puck easily so it won't get out of control. Don't lift your stick too high off the ice when you stop the puck with the blade's other side.

Keep the puck out in front of you at all times with your head up so you can see what is going on. Do not keep the puck too close to your feet. If you do, you are going to have to lower your head to watch it. And with your head down watching the puck, you have a great chance of getting a hard check and going on the injured list.

While carrying the puck out front, you are in position to pass right or left.

Do not travel with the puck beside you because you are only able to pass off in one direction. Leave the puck out front so you can go either way and nobody will be able to sweep the puck from you coming up from behind.

Passing the puck is similar to wrist shooting. Do not slap the puck, sweep it across the ice to your teammate. Keep your head up. Do not look up just before you pass and then drop it down again. This is the exact time when an opposing player could skate between you and your own man and pick off a pass.

A pass that is made too soft can also be easily stolen. All passes should be steady and strong. Your passing target is your player's stick. Aim for it. If he is expecting a pass, his stick will be down. Passing is like shooting ducks. You lead the duck—so, when you are skating, lead the pass to your man.

Most important: Keep your head up at all times. Never attempt a head-down pass. You not only could get hit real hard, but you will not be able to keep track of the other players.

When receiving a pass, keep your stick out in front so the player has a target to aim at. When the puck hits your stick, cradle or cushion it. Let your stick give just a little so the puck will not bounce right off. If your stick is held too stiffly the puck will hit it and fly off.

CHECKING

The defensive moves of blocking a player out of play or "stealing" and regaining possession of the puck are called checking.

STICK-CHECKING is covered in detail by the photos, so study them carefully. There are three basic forms of stick-checking: the sweep, the hook, and the poke. They all require constant practice.

BODY-CHECKING, again the pictures tell the story. The body-check is only permitted with the shoulder and hip, and only two strides toward the puck-carrier are allowed. When checking a man, you do not have to knock him down or put him over the boards. Checking a man is simply taking him out of the play.

The proper way to take a man out on the boards—stay ahead of him.

Right Way. As you can see in the pictures, I am letting my opponent come to me. I stay half a stride ahead of him and work into his body to tie him up.

Tie your man up on the boards and make sure he does not get away.

I am too far behind my man, so he is able to push me away.

Wrong Way. I have let the man get a half-step ahead of me and then tried to check him. All he does is push me away from him and you can see that I am trying to check him from behind.

My opponent is pushing me away from him.

SHOULDER-CHECK

Lower your body so that you will catch your man in the chest area with your shoulder (see picture). I have reduced my body height so that I can aim my shoulder around his chest and take him out of the play or at least knock him off balance.

Note how my eyes are focused on his chest.

Close-up of a proper hip-check.

HIP-CHECK

You let your man come to you and then get your hip into him. The hip-check is commonly used when you have a man near the boards.

If you catch a player at center ice with a hip-check, you can be sure of giving him a real jolt. When checking an opponent, you do not have to knock him down. If he is put out of the play, he has been checked.

POKE-CHECK

The poke-check is one of the most common methods of interfering with the progress of a puck-carrier. Let the man come to you and try not to commit yourself too soon or you can be easily deked.

If you miss your man, you are in trouble because he is coming toward you and traveling at a much greater speed.

From the photos you can see that I am near enough to my man to reach him with a poke-check. My stick is close to my body and extended at full length, and I poke the puck off his stick.

69

Waiting for my man to come to me so I can apply a poke-check.

Extending my stick full length—second motion of a successful poke-check.

Poking the puck off his stick.

The puck is now out of his control.

SWEEP-CHECK

As in all stick-checking, wait for your man to come to you. Have the stick close to your body and ready to reach out at your opponent. If you miss, you will be beaten quite easily. One split second is all that he needs to pass you.

As he approaches, wait until you can reach him with your extended stick. Put the stick flat on the ice. Use it just like a broom. Sweep the puck away.

Sweep-checks are useful when your man has gotten ahead of you. Try to catch up with him, reach from behind, then clear the puck aside.

74

Sweep-check—waiting for opponent to get close enough.

Reaching out with my stick flat on the ice.

Commencing the sweeping motion.

Pulling the puck away from the man.

The puck now swept into the corner and out of an opponent's control.

FORE-CHECK

(Photo 1) The puck is shot into the corner, and I am making sure that the man is going into the corner and not back up along the boards.

(Photo 2) He has started behind the net. I am not going too close to the goal because if I did he might be able to stop when he reaches X (MARKED ON PHOTO). If I am too far here where ARROW (MARKED ON PHOTO) is, he will stop, dash back out this way, and be gone.

(Photo 3) I am positive that he is heading behind the net.

(Photo 4) To be at O (MARKED ON PHOTO) would be wrong. He would stop because he is going faster than I, duck inside again, and beat me clean.

(Photo 5) **The man is in the corner, just where I want him.**

(Photo 6) Gradually I work into him, taking him out of the play with my body always in front of his.

BACK-CHECK

Skating back with your man is called back-checking. Always watch your wing man: you have got to skate back with him, keeping him between the boards and yourself. Stay at least a half-stride ahead but not too far advanced or he will duck in behind you. If he gets a step on you, he can cut in and push you out of the way and scoot into center ice. If he gets away and you start tripping or hooking, a penalty will be called.

When back-checking, always keep your stick out in front of you. Sometimes the opposition may try a pass, but with your stick out you can block it. Never turn your back on the man you are back-checking. If your opponent happens to get the puck, force him into the corner and take him out of the play.

DEFENDING THE GOAL

(Photo 1) The puck is in the corner of the goal I am defending. Unfortunately, I have let the man get in front of me. He should be behind. The opponent's back is to me and his shoulder is turned the other way. Should anyone shoot the puck over in that direction, he can deflect it or even get a clear shot at the net by pushing me out of the way with his hip or shoulder.

(Photo 2) Here the man is all tied up. I can still watch the puck and the corner and keep an eye on my man in front of the net.

BLOCKING SHOTS

Before you attempt to block a shot, be sure that your opponent is going to shoot the puck. If you drop and he fakes his shot, you will be down and out of position.

To block a shot on one knee, drop down to one knee and stretch your stick out in front. If you are deked, you still might be able to poke- or sweep-check the puck away. With only one knee on the ice, you can get back up much faster than if you were blocking on both knees.

To block a shot on two knees, hit the ice with both knees, again with the stick out front ready for a sweep- or poke-check. When down on two knees you are actually throwing your body directly at the man shooting. Your arms must be close to your body to present the largest blocking area possible. If your arms are not close to your body, the opponent can shoot the puck between your body and arms. More than likely your goaltender will not see the puck coming and it could mean a red light (goal).

89

Fall on one or two knees near enough to the puck-carrier so that his shot will not rise and sail over you. If you are not alert the puck could lift into your face. Be careful.

Before you drop to block, watch the deke, watch the puck, and be sure the man is going to shoot.

Starting a two-knee blocking move as my man gets set to shoot.

My stick is out front and my body is going into the shot.

Down on both knees with arms close to side to present largest blocking area possible.

92

Starting a one-knee block as my opponent starts to shoot.

94

Arms at my side, stick down on ice, with one knee down.

PLAYING DEFENSE

Keys to diagrams: **X** (puck-carrier), x (forwards), • (defensemen)

① TWO-ON-ONE: Lone defenseman hopes the puck-carrier will move in direction of arrow and shoot from this spot. Defenseman has to keep eye on both players at once. Goaltender will play the puck-carrier.

② THREE-ON-ONE: Here the single defenseman has to watch all three opponents at the same time. Goaltender again concentrates on the puck-carrier.

③ THREE-ON-TWO: Left defenseman will watch the right forward, the right defenseman will have to take care of the puck-carrier and the center man. Goaltender watches the puck-carrier.

④ TWO-ON-TWO: Left defenseman takes care of the right forward, the right defenseman goes after the puck-carrier. Again the goaltender's attention is on the puck-carrier.

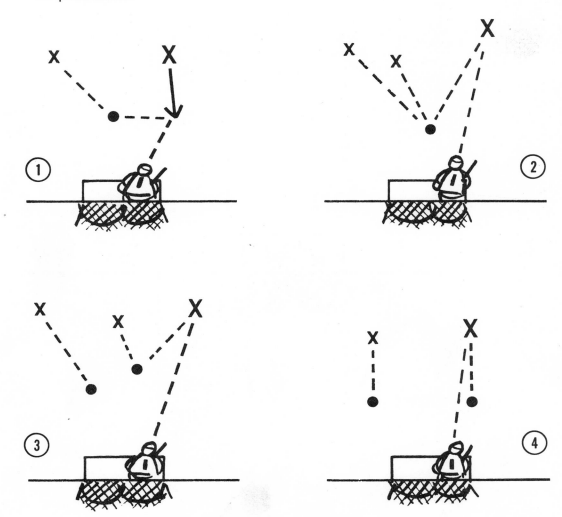

PENALTY KILLING

When our team is killing a penalty, we line up in a box formation (see drawing). What we are trying to do is keep the puck and the opponents outside the square. Our men attempt to get the puck down to the other end and keep it there, for even a possible shorthanded score. The opponent, having a one-man advantage, will be concentrating on offense.

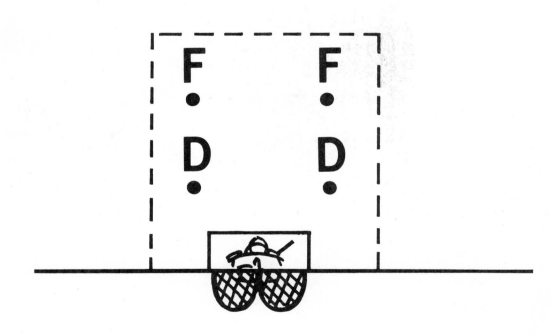

DEKING—FAKING

Basically there are three dekes.

Head-Deke
Drop your head one way, move the other.

Shoulder-Deke
Drop your shoulder one way, move the other.

Stick-Deke
Hold it one way, leave the puck, move the other way.

Your feet are very important in deking. You must be able to pivot back and forth. Fast feet are necessary when an opposing player has caught your deke. You must be ready to skate in the opposite direction. In deking, like everything else, only practice makes it near perfect.

To defend against the deke, keep your eyes glued steadily on your opponent's chest. Players can move their heads and shoulders in one way and go the other, but their chests have to ride with the rest of the body. By watching your opponent like this, you are set to (A) take him out, (B) use a sweep-check, and (C) come up with a poke-check. And you will still see most of the players on the ice.

PENALTIES

These pictures show some of the more common penalties. Penalties usually are called because the player at fault gets lazy. You are not back-checking, or you have been caught out of position. So you start grabbing, holding, or hooking. You get desperate because your opponent has gotten away.

This is tripping, a minor penalty.

An elbow in the face brings two minutes in the penalty box.

100

Hooking—two minutes.

Holding—another minor penalty.

This is cross-checking—two minutes in the penalty box.

OTHER PENALTIES

INTERFERENCE: interfering with the progress of an opponent who does not have the puck. A minor penalty.

CHARGING: running, jumping, or charging an opponent. Can be either a minor or major penalty.

SLASHING: impeding the progress of another player by "slashing" with a stick. A minor or major penalty can be given. You cannot swing your stick at another player during any altercation. If you do, you can be subject to a match penalty plus even a large fine and suspension.

HIGH-STICKING: carrying the stick above shoulder level stops the play and a face-off is held right at the spot. Either a minor or major penalty is called.

BOARDING: causing an opponent to crash heavily into the boards. If the opponent is not the puck-carrier, a minor or major penalty will be handed out.

SPEARING: stabbing an opponent with the point of the stick blade. Minor, major, or match penalty can be called.

BUTT-ENDING: hitting a man with the butt of the stick, with both hands on the stick and no part of the stick on the ice. Minor or major.

FIGHTING: starting a fight. A major, double minor, or minor penalty may be handed out. The man who retaliates usually gets a minor call.

ROUGHING: unnecessary roughness used on another player. Minor penalty.

PLAYING WITH A BROKEN STICK: minor penalty.

THROWING A STICK: if the defending team throws a stick at the puck and no goal is scored after play has been completed. A penalty shot is awarded to the opposition. A major penalty is given to the player who throws his stick.

HANDLING PUCK WITH HANDS: closing hand on puck (except for goalie) gets a minor penalty.

FALLING ON THE PUCK: deliberately falling on the puck (except for goalie). Minor penalty.

FACE-OFF VIOLATION: making physical contact with opponent's body during face-off. Minor penalty.

EQUIPMENT VIOLATION: wearing illegal equipment. Minor.

DELAY OF GAME: bench minor for team that causes unnecessary delays or has too many men on the ice at once.

BENCH MINOR: removal for 2 minutes of one player of the team against which the penalty is called. Any player may serve the penalty.

103

MAJOR PENALTY: for the first major penalty in a game, the man is ruled off ice for 5 minutes—no substitute is allowed. If he gets a second major penalty, he goes to the penalty box for 15 minutes but a substitute is allowed after 5 minutes. Should the same player draw a third major in the same game, he is expelled from the contest but a substitute can go on the ice after 5 minutes have gone by. In the NHL, a fine may also be attached to a major penalty.

MISCONDUCT: is for 10 minutes, usually for abusive language or gestures. However, his team does not play shorthanded. In pro hockey, an automatic fine accompanys the penalty.

GAME MISCONDUCT: suspension of player from balance of the game. A substitute is permitted as a replacement.

MATCH PENALTY: game ejection for (1) deliberate attempt to injure—substitute can skate after 5 minutes, (2) deliberate injury to an opponent, in which case the team plays shorthanded for 10 minutes. NHL match penalties usually bring further suspensions and fines.

PENALTY SHOT: player on one team gets a clear shot at the opponent's goal and goaltender. Penalty shot is awarded when one man carrying the puck is illegally impeded from behind with no opponent (except the goaltender) between him and opponent's goal. Penalty shot is also awarded when any defender, other than the goaltender, falls on the puck in the defending goal crease.

GOALTENDER PENALTY: all goaltenders' penalties—minor, major, misconduct—must be served by another team member. If a goaltender receives a game misconduct or a match penalty, his place in goal must be taken by a substitute.

GOALTENDING

I would say that the goaltender is one of the most valuable players on the team. He has to be exceptionally alert and agile for a full 60 minutes of every game.

When he is in the ready position his feet are wide enough apart to keep the pads closed. His knees must be slightly bent to allow quick movements right and left. The goaltender's body is bent forward at the waist, putting his eyes close to ice level with his stick kept flat on the ice in front of the skates. The stick is held in one hand while the other is ready to catch a flying puck.

Constantly watching the action, the goaltender moves from side to side with his body concentrated on the puck's position.

Goaltenders use special skates with a flat, low blade for both better balance and stopping the puck from sneaking between the blade and the shoe boot. Leg pads are 10 inches wide and give cover from the ankles to above the knees. He also wears a heavy felt chest-protector for his abdomen, shoulders, and arms. His catching-hand glove is well padded for extra protection. Most goalies also use face masks. The total equipment weighs approximately 40 pounds, about double the weight the other players carry.

The goaltender in full uniform, Eddie Johnston of the Boston Bruins.

Another photo of goaltender equipment.

Exercise for a goaltender playing without a stick following teammate's hand directions. Goaltenders must think and act quickly.

PRACTICE FOR THE GOALTENDER

Moving the goalie left in a practice session.

Coming forward out of net following hand signals.

Goaltender going to his right, still without a stick.

Getting up fast after falling down.

Coming out and going back fast into his net.

Hitting the ice with both knees.

Attempting to stop a pass out from behind the net, the goaltender watches the man behind the net with his stick ready to poke the puck away.

Man makes pass behind net, and goaltender follows puck and knocks it away from second man waiting in front of net.

115

Puck is being knocked away from net.

Goaltender clears puck away from net.

That's Frosty Forristall, Bruins' assistant trainer, sounding off about how hard he works and what an easy life the players have. Dan Canney, our head trainer, is lacing on his shoes for another full day's work.

THE TEAM TRAINERS

The trainers in pro hockey deserve great credit. In Boston we have an excellent head trainer, Dan Canney, and his capable assistant, John "Frosty" Forristall.

Dan is the man who performs all the treatment miracles on injuries. When a player pulls up with ailments, the head trainer gets out his therapeutic devices and things get better again.

Frosty takes care of all our equipment—packing, unpacking, cleaning, drying, hanging, picking up, and repairing. If you need extra protection for a bad bruise, our trainers get the padding added in the right places.

Our team does extensive traveling to keep pace with our heavy NHL schedule. This puts an extra burden on the trainers, checking plane departures and keeping tabs on the equipment. Many a night I have seen both men going to various rinks at three and four in the morning to check our equipment. Trainers are vital cogs on any team.

TYPICAL GAME DAY

The night before a game in Boston, my roommates and I usually attend a movie. We get home around eleven. If we are tired, we will hit the sack right away. If not, we will stay up for a while watching TV. Many a night you may find yourself tossing and turning in bed, thinking about the team you will play the next evening.

On game day the squad usually checks into the Garden dressing room around ten in the morning. Some of the boys with injuries receive treatments. Others tape their sticks and check their equipment. Of course, the ice is always available for skating, so usually the players who don't get too much game time will work out.

After leaving the Garden, I may go shopping or visit some friends. Then I head back home, where we usually eat dinner between one-thirty and two in the afternoon. After eating I take a little nap. Some of the other players on the team like to relax at afternoon movies. If the game is scheduled for seven-thirty at night we have to be in the dressing room one hour before the warm-up. I get in early to recheck my sticks, shoot the breeze, and take it easy before going on the ice. The Bruins get on the ice about a half-hour before the face-off. We have a 15-minute warmup, which consists of skating and taking shots at the goaltender. Just before and during the game we do not drink any fluids. You should not drink water because it will bloat you with a heavy-stomach feeling. Water might also give you cramps during a game. Between periods we sit in the dressing room planning game strategy and talking over mistakes made during the period just played. Then back out on the ice until the final buzzer sounds.

Mornings before a game we often go into the Garden for some skating exercise.

Shopping—one muskrat coat, one sealskin coat, two hockey players (the other one is Eddie Johnston), and one furrier.

Bruin teammate Gary Doak and I checking game schedules.

Most hockey players are big steak eaters.

We eat our game-day meals about one or two in the afternoon.

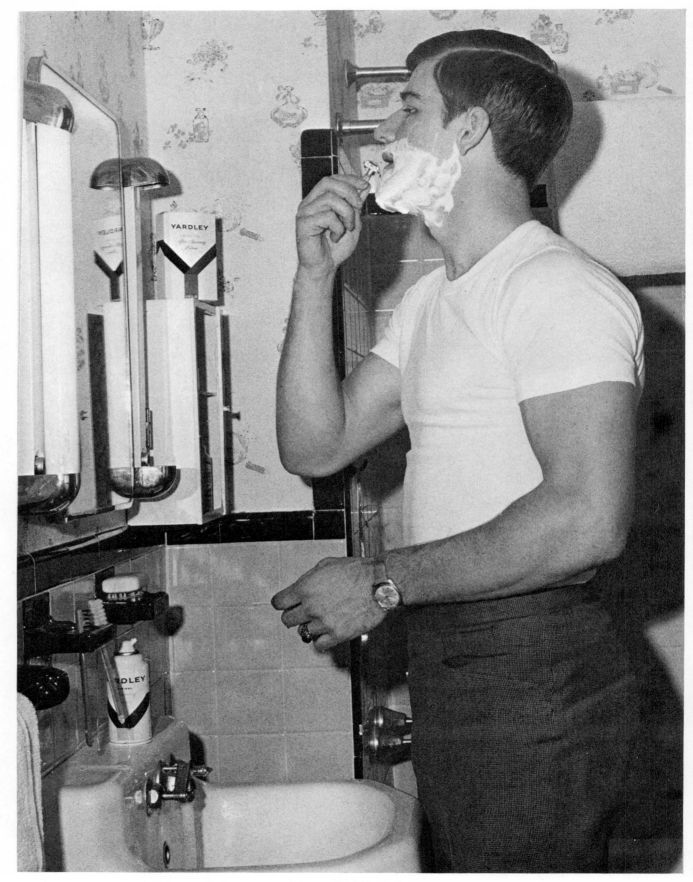

Shaving before a game.

Roommate, Frosty Forristall and I getting ready to drive to Boston for a game.

I like to get in the dressing room early so I can catch up on mail from my young fans.

Time to shoot the breeze with some of the people who drop in—this is Woody Dumart, former Boston star who now supplies us with equipment.

Not all my friends are hockey players. This is Julia Donahue getting ready to enjoy a post-game dinner.

I guess we travel over 50,000 miles a season.

BOBBY ORR-MIKE WALTON SPORTS CAMP

The Bobby Orr-Mike Walton Sports Camp is located on the shores of Lake Couchiching in Orillia, Canada. I am a partner of Toronto Maple Leafs' center, Mike Walton, in the camp complex. The camp comprises 180 acres with two miles of sandy-beach lake frontage.

The summer of 1969 was our first camp and we had nine weekly sessions of camping for boys between the ages of seven to fourteen. We hope to accommodate up to one thousand boys throughout a summer season.

Mike Walton and I teach hockey on a full-time basis and we have Bill Watters, B.Ph.Ed., in charge of the whole operation as camp director. Several NHL players serve as assistants in the hockey program and ten other live-in instructors are on hand for the waterfront and land activities.

Administration at the camp is handled by another partner, Bob Haggert, who has been connected with hockey for over twenty years. Formerly with the Toronto Maple Leaf organization, Bob is now president of Sports Representatives Ltd. in Toronto.

Campers receive a thoroughly supervised program of waterfront and land sports. Qualified instructors teach the fundamentals of boating and water safety. The boys also learn the proper method of entering a canoe and get their first instruction in water-skiing.

Enrollment is divided into four sections according to age and hockey-playing ability. The youngsters begin every morning at seven with a short run before a hearty breakfast.

Morning and afternoon curriculum calls for the four groups to move between various hockey, field, and waterfront areas. Each camper receives at least an hour and three-quarters of ice time each day in our indoor arena.

Bedtime is at nine in the evening. Sleeping accommodations are on the second floor of the main lodge. We put four boys in double bunks in one room with adjoining washroom facilities.

Richard is one of the 1,000 boys who attend my sports camp every summer.

The sports camp offers youngsters a well-rounded outdoor life on land and water.

OFF SEASON

Before I started a boys summer camp with Mike Walton, I used to spend most of the summer relaxing in my hometown, Parry Sound, Ontario. Fishing, swimming, and water-skiing took up much of my time. But now, I spend all of July and August working with hundreds of youngsters from all over the United States and Canada. In my free moments I devote time to my various business enterprises. I also manage to play in a few golf tournaments and relax with friends I do not see all winter. Before you know it, Labor Day rolls around and another hockey year is on the calendar.

Ward Cornell, Canadian sportscaster, and Sandra Post, one of Canada's top women golfers.

Water-skiing—a great summer sport.

Real workout—washing Brutus, a nonswimmer.

THE BOBBY ORR HOCKEY SHOW

The Hockey Show is put on a few times each winter at various ice arenas in Massachusetts. It gives me and some of the other Bruins a chance to meet thousands of youngsters who might not be able to attend a Boston NHL game at the Garden.

We usually schedule an actual professional hockey practice. We demonstrate power plays, team passing, stick-handling, skating, shooting, and goaltending. Hockey players from surrounding high schools are selected by their coaches, and they skate on the ice with us throughout the show. In the final segment, they scrimmage against our club. The high school boys have been tough opponents, but so far we still have a perfect record.

A meet-the-players autograph session takes place for half-an-hour before each show giving young fans and parents a chance to meet some of the Bruins in person. Time for questions and answers is taken midway through the evening. After the show, lucky ticket holders are awarded signed hockey sticks used by the Bruins in the program.

Autograph time during the Bobby Orr Hockey Show.

AND NOW THE GAME

Ranger goaltender is going down, and I am about to use the flip shot.

I am a step ahead of my man, and he is in trouble.

Blocking a man out of play.

Defending the goal, keeping my man from getting close in.

Shooting from a tough angle against Toronto.

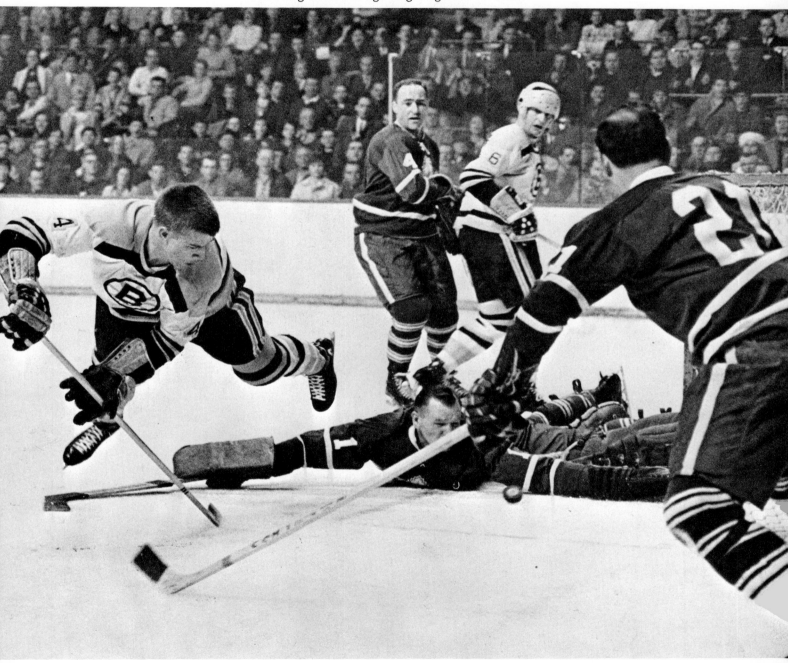

Trying a slap shot. As I said, they are not always accurate.

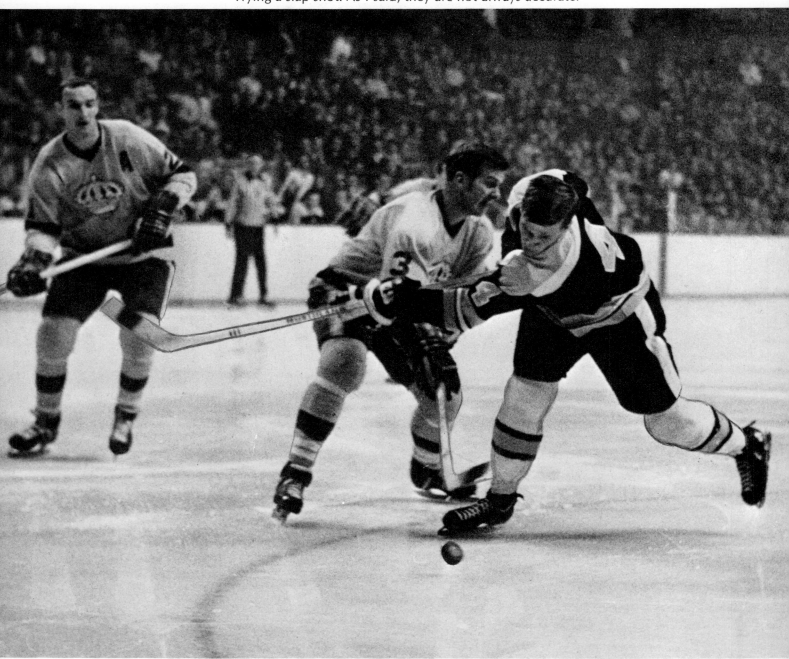

Controlling the puck behind our net and starting a rush up ice.

If it was not on a hockey rink, I'd swear this was a golf shot.

Head up, puck out front, setting up a pass to a teammate.

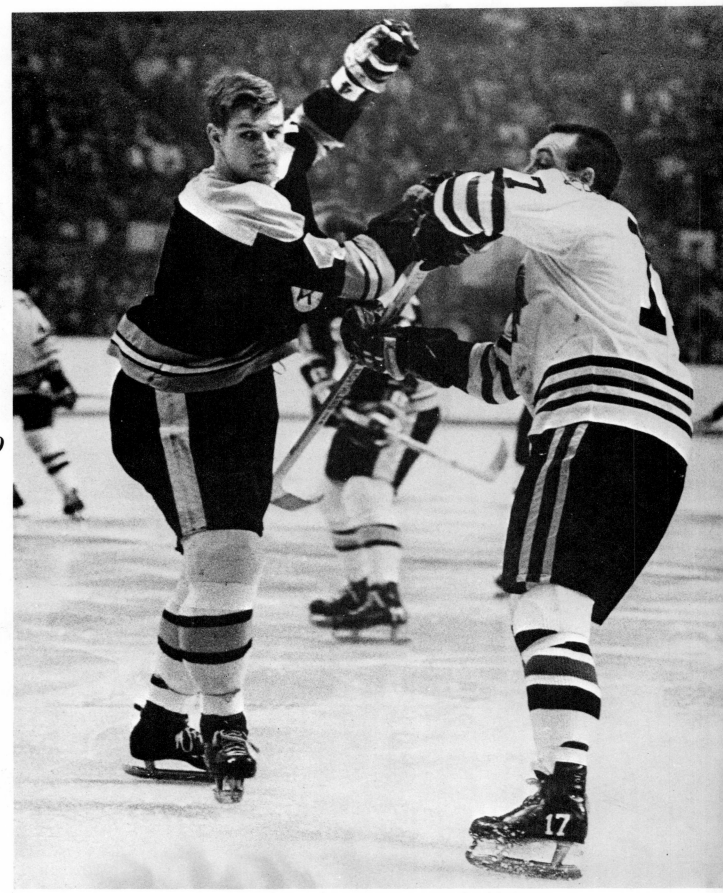

Once in a while we have a dance, even with a black eye.

Approaching the Chicago goal in a down-on-the-ice manner.

Closer and closer to the goal.

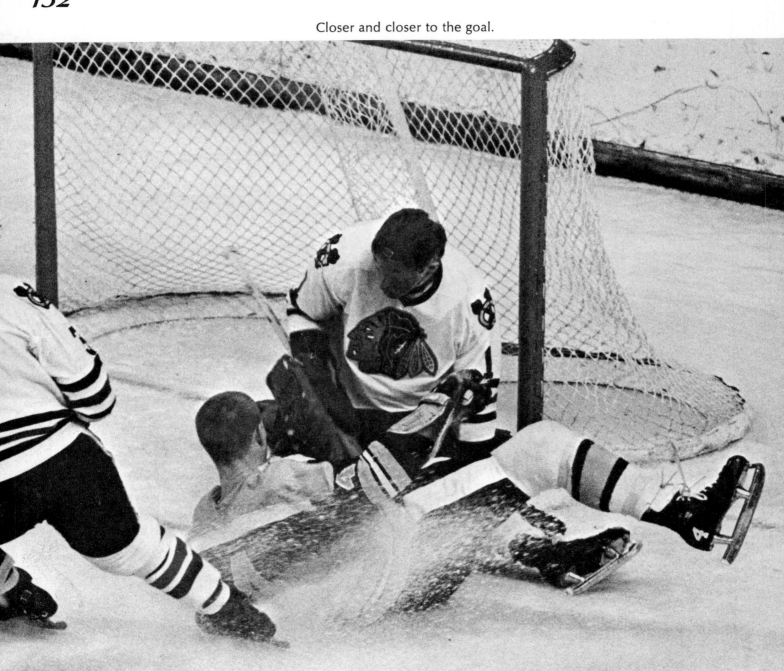

Believe it or not, I actually scored on this play surrounded by Black Hawks and sticks.

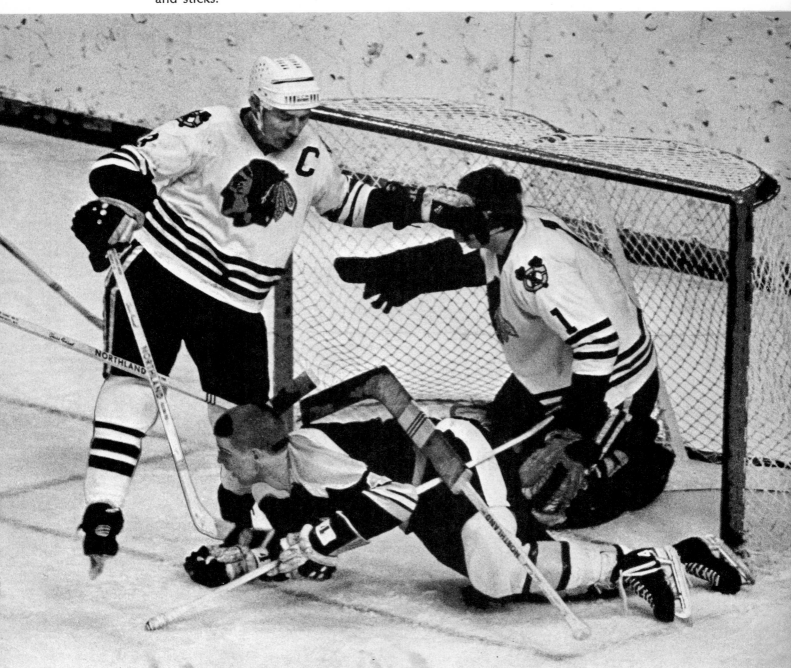

THE HOCKEY RINK

The professional hockey rink is 200 x 85 feet and is a round-cornered rectangle enclosed by wooden boards 3½ to 4 feet high. Wire screen or special durable glass is fastened on top of the boards for game-viewing protection.

Ten feet from each end of the rink is a 2-inch red goal line that spreads across the ice. The goal measures 6 feet in length and 4 feet in height and is centered on each goal line. The goal crease is 8 feet in width and extends 4 feet from the line of the goal.

The area between both goals is divided into three segments by two 12-inch-wide blue lines. Each blue line is parallel to the goals and 60 feet in front of it. A 12-inch-wide red line cuts the rink ice in half-sections.

All zones (attacking, defending, and neutral) and face-off spots are designated on the diagram on this page.

154   Players' benches, with room for fourteen men, are alongside the ice, in the neutral zone and as close as possible to the center of the rink. Each rink must be provided with benches or seats called a Penalty Bench. Immediately in front of the penalty timekeeper's seat is a semicircle, 10 feet in radius and 2 inches wide, known as the Referee's Crease.

Behind each goal is a stationary red light that is illuminated when a goal is scored at that end. Buzzers and green lights signify the end of a period and a game.

An electrical timepiece keeps fans, players, and officials informed of all time elements throughout the game.

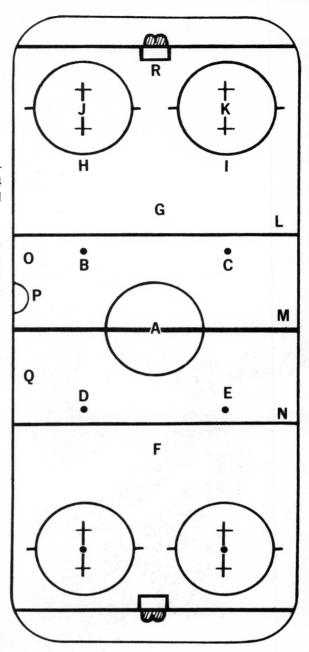

DIAGRAM KEYS

A–Center Ice Circle Face-Off Spot
B–Face-Off Spot
C–Face-Off Spot
D–Face-Off Spot
E–Face-Off Spot
F–Attacking Zone
G–Defending Zone
H–Restraining Circle
I–Restraining Circle
J–Face-Off Spot
K–Face-Off Spot
L–Blue Line
M–Center Line
N–Blue Line
O–Neutral Zone
P–Referee's Crease
Q–Neutral Zone

TEAM LINEUP

The official lineup calls for six players on each team. They are: a goaltender, two defensemen (left and right), two wings (left and right), and a center.

The forward line is composed of the center and two wings, who play together as a unit. Defensemen are also paired in units.

The time that forwards and defensemen spend on the ice varies. The goaltender usually plays a full sixty minutes in each game.

Most NHL teams retain three complete lines, two defensemen pairings, two goaltenders, a fifth defenseman, and a couple of spare skaters who are used for killing off penalties and other odd jobs.

All players must be dressed uniformly. Individual identifying numbers at least 10 inches high must appear on backs of jerseys.

Each team should have a playing captain and not more than three alternate captains.

A substitute goaltender, fully dressed and equipped, must be ready to play at all times.

155

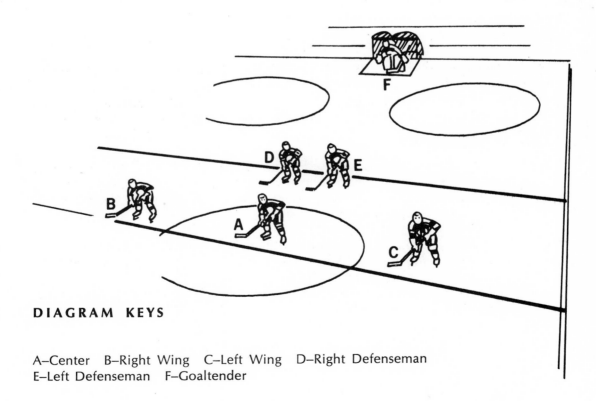

DIAGRAM KEYS

A–Center B–Right Wing C–Left Wing D–Right Defenseman
E–Left Defenseman F–Goaltender

ICING

Icing is called when a player on a team equal or superior in numerical strength shoots, bats, or deflects the puck from his own half of the ice, beyond the goal line of the opposing team. "Icing The Puck" is completed the instant a defending player (other than the goaltender) touches the puck (see X on the diagram).

Play is stopped and the puck faced-off at the end face-off spot of the offending team. However, play is not stopped if the puck enters the opponent's net, in which case it is a goal. What would be icing—as described above—is not enforced if a team is playing shorthanded.

If a linesman believes an opponent could have played the puck before it crossed his goal line, he will not call an icing. Also, in case the puck goes over any section of the goal crease, no icing is called.
The game continues without a whistle if an icing team member touches the puck before an opponent reaches it.

(X) indicates attacking-team member has crossed over defending team's blue line before the puck.

OFFSIDE

An offside takes place when a player of the puck-carrying team goes into the attacking zone before the puck. Play stops and a face-off takes place in the neutral zone at the face-off spot nearest the attacking zone of the offending team.

Skates and not sticks decide all offsides. A player is offside when both skates are completely over the outer edge of the determining center line or blue line involved in the play.

If the linesman decides an intentional offside play has been made, the puck will be faced-off at the end face-off spot in the defending zone of the offending team.

THE OFFSIDE PASS

An offside pass is called when a player in one zone passes the puck forward to a teammate in another zone. However, this can be done by a player on the

X

Offside Pass: man is passing the puck from one zone to a teammate in another zone. (X) indicates direction of opponent's goal.

defending team, which can make and take forward passes from their own defending zone to the center line.

The "forward pass" from the defending zone must be completed by the pass-receiver, who is legally onside at the center line.

Players on the attacking team must not precede the puck into the attacking zone. If this happens, play is stopped and the puck is faced-off in the neutral zone at the face-off spot nearest the attacking zone of the offending team.

PUCK OUT-OF-BOUNDS AND UNPLAYABLE

If the puck leaves the ice surface, it must be faced-off at the location of the shot or deflection.

When the puck hangs in the netting or outside the goal, the puck can be played off the back of the net.

When the referee loses sight of the puck he stops the play with his whistle. Face-offs take place at the exact location where play stopped.

He also stops play when the puck is "frozen" along the boards between opponents. The puck is faced-off at either of the nearby face-off areas.

All play stoppages caused by the attacking team require face-offs in the neutral zone.

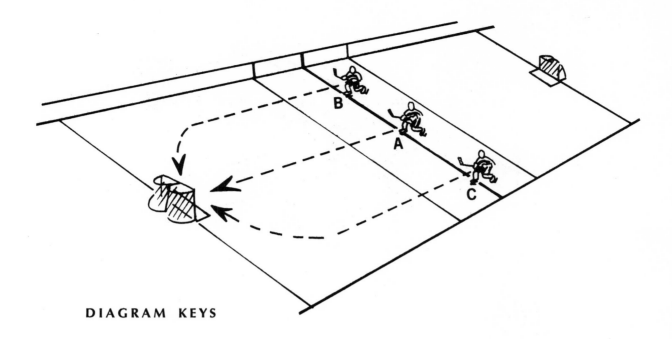

DIAGRAM KEYS

A—Center skating down the middle section
B—Right wing covering the right lane
C—Left wing patrolling the left lane

159

THE OFFENSE

The attacking members of any team are the forwards—the center and his two wing men. Three imaginary sections or lanes divide the ice for the skating offense. The left and right wings skate up and down the outside lanes, and the center patrols the middle. It is the major function of the center and wings to carry the puck forward into the opponent's defensive zone (see diagram).

There are a few exceptions, but the majority of wings are the fastest skaters and hardest shooters in hockey clubs. Most left wings shoot left-handed while the right wings usually shoot from the right side of their bodies.

Centers handle almost all the face-off assignments.

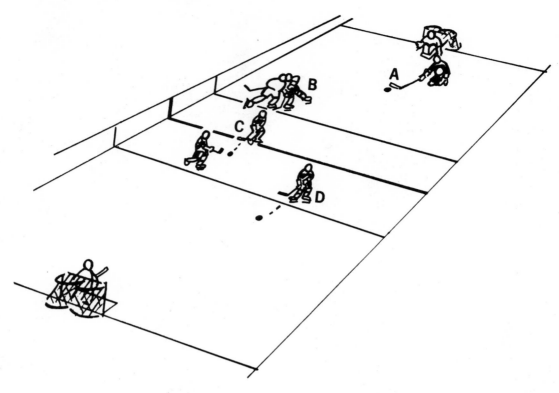

DIAGRAM KEYS

A–Defenseman blocks shots with stick or body
B–Taking opponents out of play
C–Defenseman passes puck up the ice to his forwards
D–Defenseman shoots on opponent's net from inside offensive blue line

THE DEFENSE

Defensemen are the backbone of the "defensive" team. The prime duty of the defensemen is to keep the opponents from getting close shots on their goal. Defensemen must use their sticks and bodies to block shots, and to clear the puck away from their goaltender and the net. It is also their job to keep attacking forwards out of play when they get possession of the puck.

On the offense, defensemen pass the puck to their forwards and follow up ice as rear guards, trailing the play.

Good low shooting from the points (inside the attacking blue line) is a must for all defensemen.

Boarding

Charging

Cross-Checking

Delayed Calling
Of Penalty

Elbowing

High-Sticking

Holding

Hooking

161

Icing

Interference

Misconduct

Slashing

Slow Whistle

Tripping

"Wash-Out"

OFFICIAL'S SIGNALS

BOARDING—Pounding the fist of one hand into the open palm of the other.

CHARGING—Rotating fists around one another in front of chest.

CROSS-CHECKING—A series of forward and backward motions with both fists extending from the chest.

DELAYED CALLING OF PENALTY—Referee extends arm and points once to penalized player.

ELBOWING—Tapping either elbow with the opposite hand.

HIGH-STICKING—Holding both fists, one immediately above the other, at the height of the forehead.

HOLDING—Clasping wrist with the hand well in front of the chest.

HOOKING—A series of tugging motions with both arms, as if pulling something toward the stomach.

ICING—Arms folded across the chest. When the puck is shot or deflected in such a manner as to produce a possible icing of the puck, the rear linesman will signal to his partner by raising either arm over his head (same as in "Slow Whistle"). Immediately after icing the puck has occurred, the forward linesman will respond with the same slow-whistle signal, the rear linesman will blow his whistle to stop the play, and both will give the proper icing signal.

INTERFERENCE—Crossed arms stationary in front of chest.

MISCONDUCT—Placing of both hands on hips several times and pointing to penalized player.

SLASHING—A series of chopping motions with the edge of one hand across the opposite forearm.

SLOW WHISTLE—Arm in which whistle is not held extended above head. If play returns to neutral zone without stoppage, arm is drawn down the instant the puck crosses the line.

TRIPPING—Extending right leg forward, clear of the ice, and striking it with right hand below the knee.

WASH-OUT—Both arms swung laterally across the body with palms down: (1) when used by the referee it means goal disallowed; (2) when used by linesman it means there is no icing or offside.

162

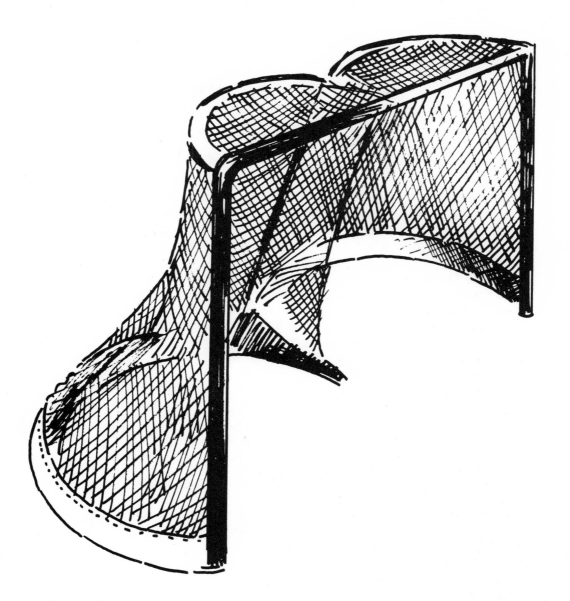

THE GOAL NET

The goal net is exactly 6 feet between posts. The posts are 2-inch-thick standard pipes and are 4 feet tall. Each is anchored to the ice with pins that extend up through the ice into the goalposts.

A crossbar of the same pipe material extends from the top of one post to that of the other. A white nylon cord netting is draped in such a manner as to prevent the puck from coming to rest on the outside.

The goalposts, crossbar, and exterior surface of other supporting framework for the goal are all painted red. The surface of the base plate inside the goal and supports other than the goalposts are white.

HOCKEY TALK

BACK CHECK—Harassment movements by the forwards skating back to their defensive zone, attempting to regain the puck from the opposition.

BACKHAND SHOT OR PASS—This is a right-handed player shooting or receiving a pass on the left side. Vice versa for a left-handed man.

BEAT THE DEFENSE—Moving past the defense into the goal.

BEAT THE GOALTENDER—Skating, shooting, and scoring on the goal.

BLIND PASS—Puck-passing without looking.

BREAK—Catching opponents out of position and starting a rush up ice.

BREAKAWAY—Puck-carrying player rushing on opponent's goal with no defensive-team member between him and goaltender.

BREAKOUT—The attacking team leaving their defensive zone and skating up the ice with the puck.

CLEARING THE PUCK—Keeping the puck away from own goal area.

COVER—A defensive player covering opponent closely in his own defensive zone so the man cannot receive a pass.

DEFLECTION—Shot or pass that hits a man or equipment and goes astray—sometimes into the net for a score.

DEKE—Faking by the puck-carrier to go around a man.

DIGGER—A hard-skating man who sticks with the puck action until he assumes control.

DOG-A-MAN—A persistent and close cover of one man on another.

FACE-OFF—An official drops the puck on the ice between two opposing players to start a game or resume action.

FEEDING—A term for puck-passing.

FLOATER—"Sleeper" is another name—a player from the offensive team who sneaks into the center zone behind the attacking defensemen.

FLOPPER—A goaltender who hits the ice too much trying to make saves.

FOUL—Breaking a rule that will bring a penalty call.

FREEZING THE PUCK—Keeping the puck jammed against the boards with a stick or skates.

GET THE JUMP—Getting a fast head start on an opponent.

ON-THE-FLY—Changing players on the ice while play is going on.

OPEN ICE—Section of the ice that has no opponent on it.

PLAYMAKER—Most often this is the center as he sets up various plays and gives directions.

POINTS—Defensemen positions on the offense inside the attacking blue line.

POWER PLAY—The team with a man advantage during a penalty sends five men into the shorthanded team's defensive zone.

PULLING THE GOALTENDER—Goaltender comes off ice to be replaced by a forward as an extra skater. A last-minute attempt to score a goal when a team is behind and the game is almost over.

RAGGING—Super stick-handling as a player keeps ownership of the puck.

REBOUND—A shot that bounces off the goaltender or his equipment.

RUSH—A player (or his team) as he carries the puck into the opponent's defensive zone.

SAVE—The goaltender stopping the puck at the goal.

SCRAMBLE—Players battling for the puck in close-range action.

SCREEN SHOT—One or more players (own team's or opponent's) as they create a screen that blocks the goaltender's vision.

SHORTHANDED—One team that has one or more players in the penalty box.

SIN-BIN—The penalty box.

SOLO—An individual rush up ice with help from a teammate.

SPLITTING THE DEFENSE—A puck-carrier breaking through two defensemen.

SPOT PASS—Passing to a certain location on ice instead of a player.

THREE-ON-ONE—Three men coming against one defensive player.

THREE-ON-TWO—Three men attacking on two defensive players.

TRAILER—One man who follows a teammate ready to receive a drop or backward pass.

TWO-ON-ONE—Two attacking men skating on one defensive man.

TWO-ON-TWO—Two attackers skating down on two defenders.

165

THE PAST, ACCOMPLISHMENTS AND FAMILY

Nine years old and a Most Valuable Player award in Parry Sound, Ontario.

168

My second year in Oshawa, 1963–64. I played for the Oshawa Generals of the Jr. A. League from 1962–66.

Signing my first Boston Bruins' contract, the Friday before Labor Day, 1966, at Lefroy, Ontario, with my attorney, Alan Eagleson.

First goal in the NHL—against Montreal in Boston, 1966–67 season.

First time back on the ice in Boston Garden after serious knee injury and operation.

Twenty-first goal scored in 1968–69, setting new NHL record for most goals scored by a defenseman.

The Orr family—left to right—my mother, sister Pat, father, sister Penny, brothers Ron and Doug.

BOBBY ORR-RECORD TO DATE

Born March 20, 1948 in Parry Sound, Ontario, Canada — 5' 11" 180 lbs

1962–1963—OSHAWA GENERALS—OHA Jr. A

GAMES	GOALS	ASSISTS	POINTS
34	6	15	21

1963–1964—OSHAWA GENERALS—OHA Jr. A

56	29	43	72

1964–1965—OSHAWA GENERALS—OHA Jr. A

56	34	59	93

1965–1966—OSHAWA GENERALS—OHA Jr. A

47	38	56	94
193	107	173	280

174

1966–1967—BOSTON BRUINS—NHL

61	13	28	41

1967–1968—BOSTON BRUINS—NHL

46	11	20	31

1968–1969—BOSTON BRUINS—NHL

67	21	43	64

1969–1970—BOSTON BRUINS—NHL

76	33	87	120

1966–1967—Won Calder Memorial Trophy as NHL Outstanding Rookie
1966–1967—Named to the second All-Star NHL Team defense
1967–1968—Won Norris Trophy as NHL Outstanding defenseman
1967–1968—Named to the first All-Star NHL Team defense
1968–1969—Won Norris Trophy (2nd consecutive time) as NHL Outstanding defenseman
1968–1969—Named to the first All-Star NHL Team defense

MOST GOALS SCORED BY A DEFENSEMAN IN A SEASON
March 20, 1969—(Orr's 21st birthday) scored record-breaking 21st goal against Chicago Black Hawks at Boston Garden, besting Flash Hollet's 20 goals made in 1944–1945.

MOST ASSISTS SCORED BY A DEFENSEMAN IN A SEASON
January 15, 1970—Scored 51st record-breaking assist at Boston Garden in a game between the Boston Bruins and the Los Angeles Kings. Former record held by Pat Stapleton of Chicago.

MOST POINTS SCORED BY A DEFENSEMAN IN A SEASON
January 19, 1970—Scored a goal and an assist for a new grand total of 65 points in a Boston Bruins 6-3 win over the Montreal Canadians at Boston Garden. Old record held by Bobby Orr, 64 points, 1968–1969.

1969–1970—Named to the first All-Star NHL Team defense—4th straight year on All-Star Team—also received every possible vote from sports writers all over United States and Canada

1969-1970—Won the Hart Trophy as NHL Most Valuable Player
1969-1970—Won Norris Trophy as NHL Outstanding Defenseman
1969-1970—Won Ross Trophy for Most Points Scored (120) in the NHL
1969-1970—Most Goals Ever Scored by a NHL Defenseman (33)
1969-1970—Most Assists Ever Scored by a NHL Player—(87)
1969-1970—Most Points Scored in 1969–1970 Season by a NHL Player—(120)

1970 STANLEY CUP SERIES

Most Points Scored by a Defenseman in NHL Stanley Cup Games (20)
Most Goals Scored by a Defenseman in NHL Stanley Cup Games (9)
Awarded Smythe Trophy as Most Valuable Player in the Stanley Cup Series

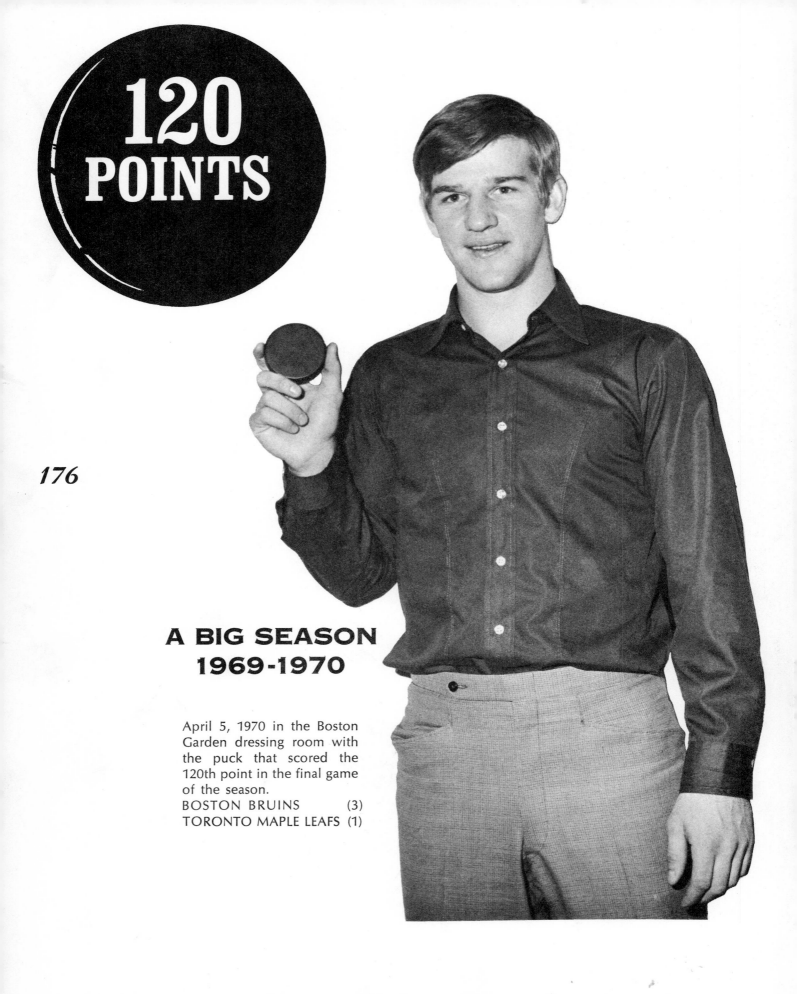

120 POINTS

176

A BIG SEASON
1969-1970

April 5, 1970 in the Boston Garden dressing room with the puck that scored the 120th point in the final game of the season.
BOSTON BRUINS (3)
TORONTO MAPLE LEAFS (1)